Mmmmm!

Sam

Sam has a hat.

Sam!

2

Sam has a mat.

Sam has a ham.

3

Get a Pet

Get a pet cat.

Peg has pets!

Get a pet rat.

Get a pet to pat.

Hop!

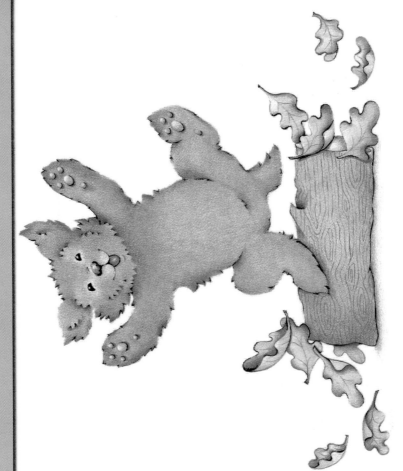

Hop on the log.

Hop, hop, hop!

Hop on the dog.

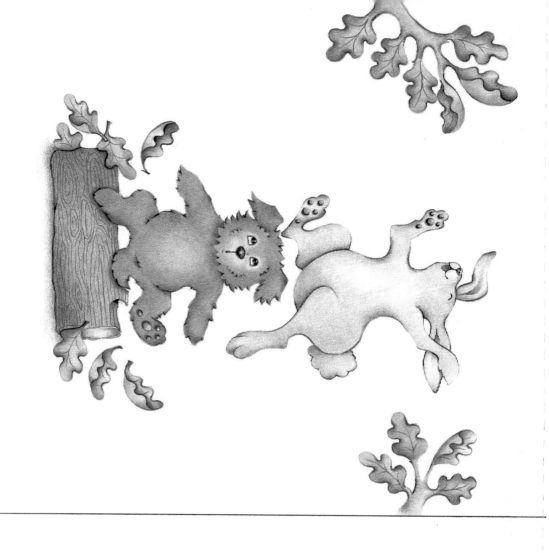

Hop on top.

Pig Hid

Pig hid in the pen
with Dad.

4

Pig hid in the bag.

Pig hid in the hat.

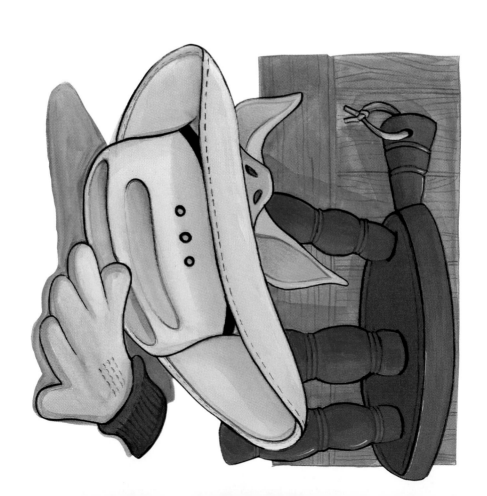

Up!

Bug went into the jam.
Yum! Yum!

4

Bug went up and up
the leg.

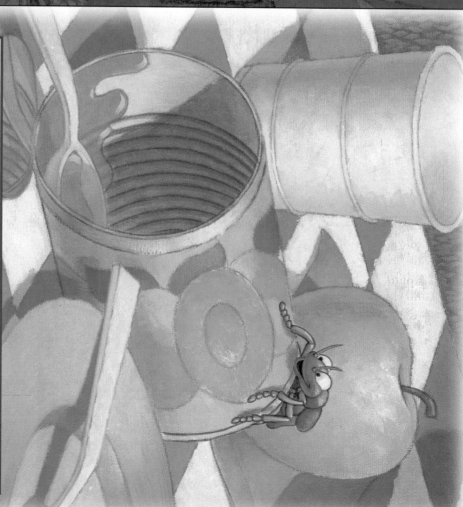

Bug went up the tin can.

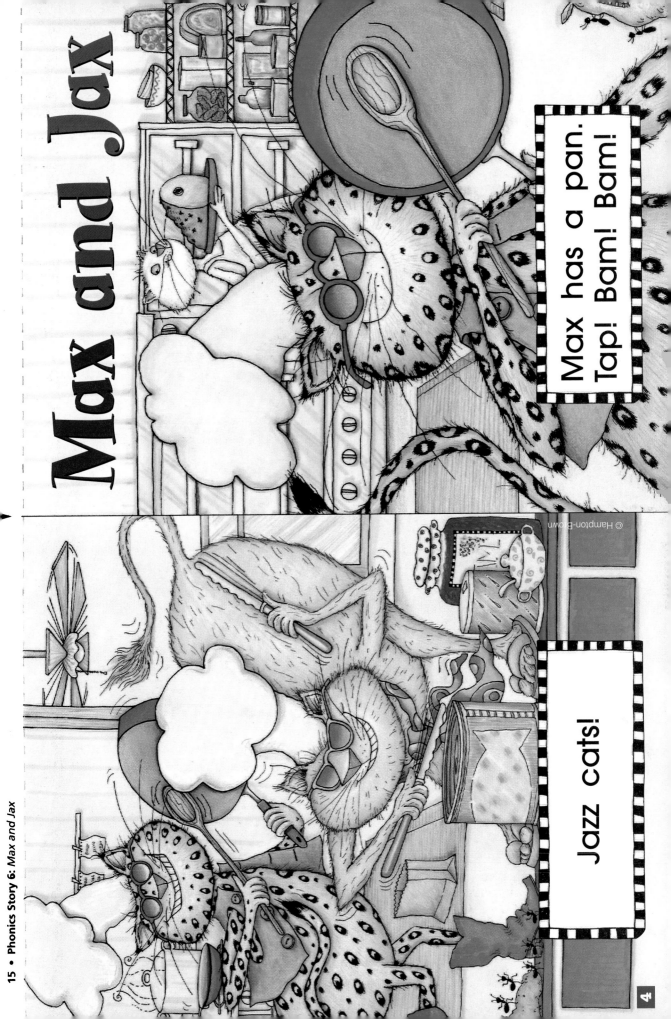

Max and Jax

Max has a pan.
Tap! Bam! Bam!

Jazz cats!

4

Jax has a can.
Rat tat tat!

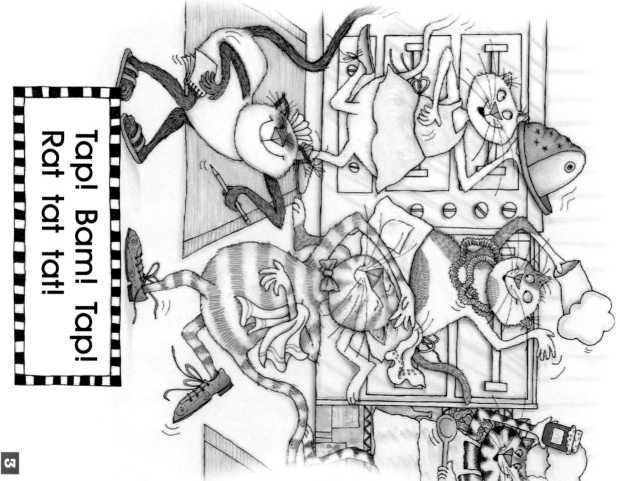

Tap! Bam! Tap!
Rat tat tat!

Get Max!

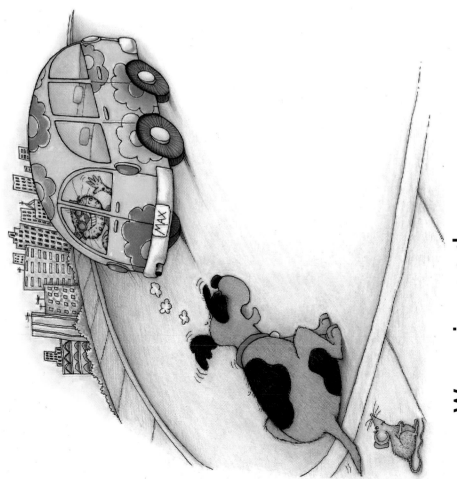

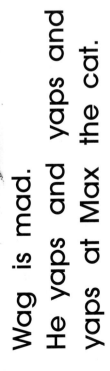

Wag is mad.
He yaps and yaps and yaps at Max the cat.

Wag likes to get Max.

Max goes to the .

Wag goes to the .

bat

fan

rat

van

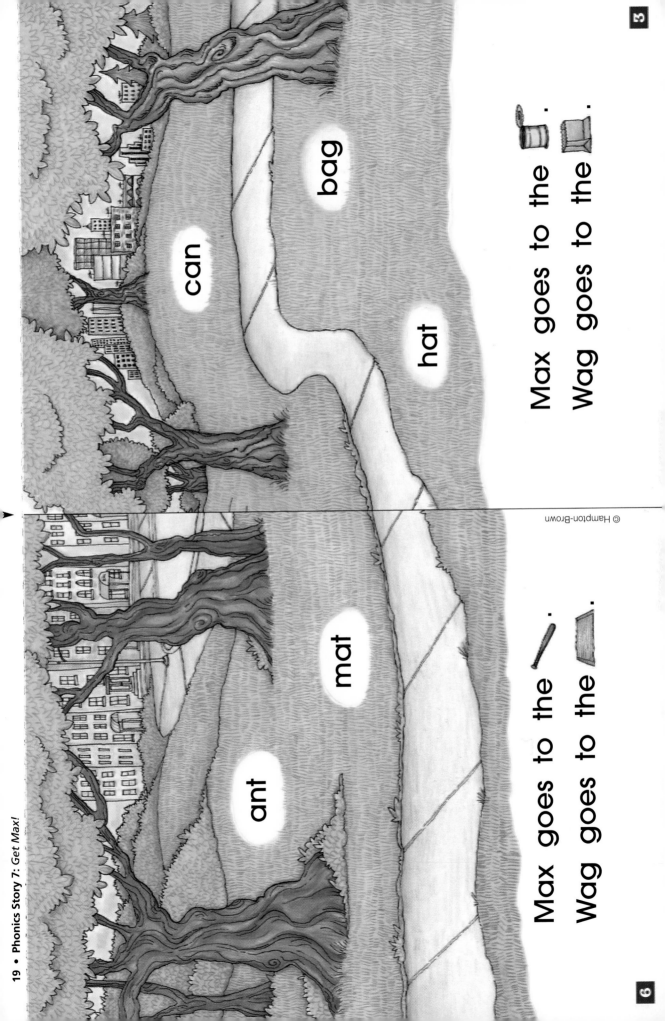

ant

mat

can

bag

hat

Max goes to the ___ .
Wag goes to the ___ .

Max goes to the ___ .
Wag goes to the ___ .

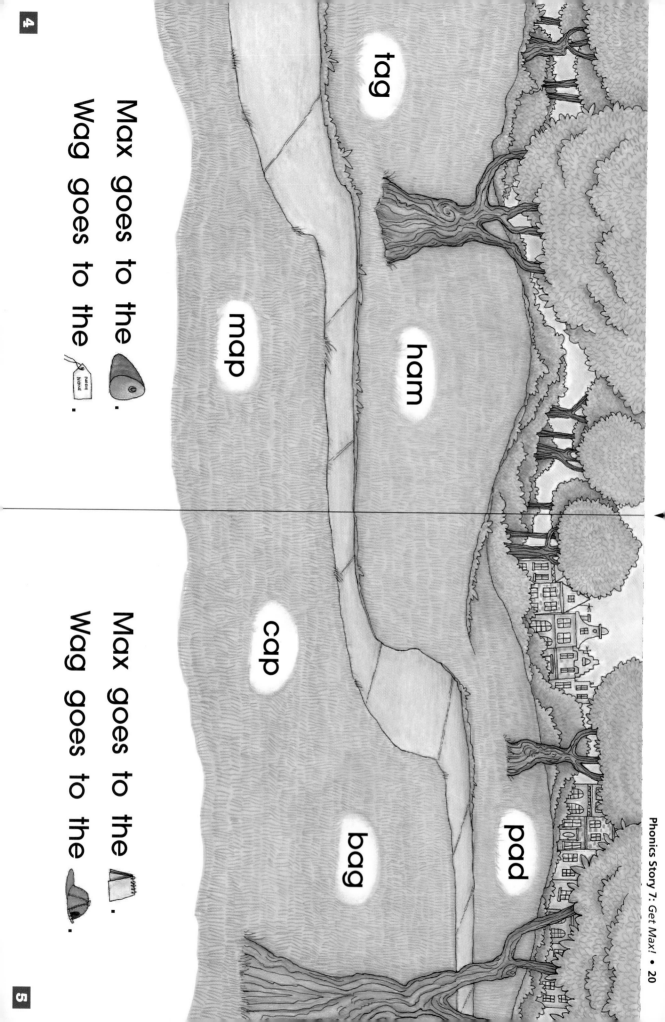

tag

map

ham

Max goes to the ●.

Wag goes to the ＊.

cap

pad

bag

Max goes to the ▲.

Wag goes to the ⬤.

NOT FUNNY, TOM!

Not funny, Tom!

Little Fox is hot.

Dog is hot.

4. pants and a top 5. pot

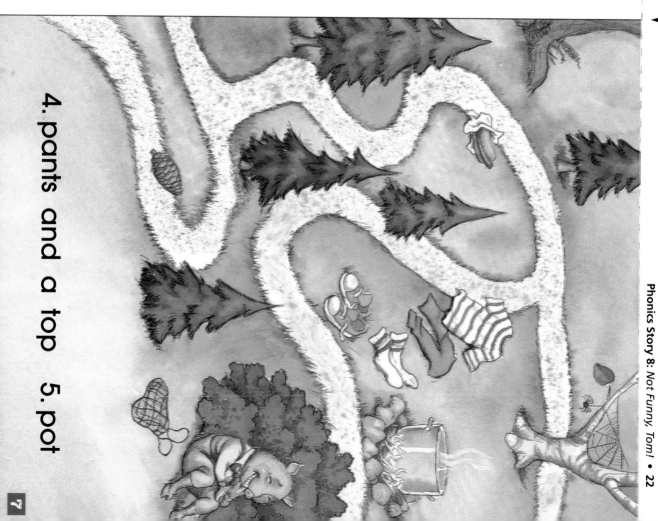

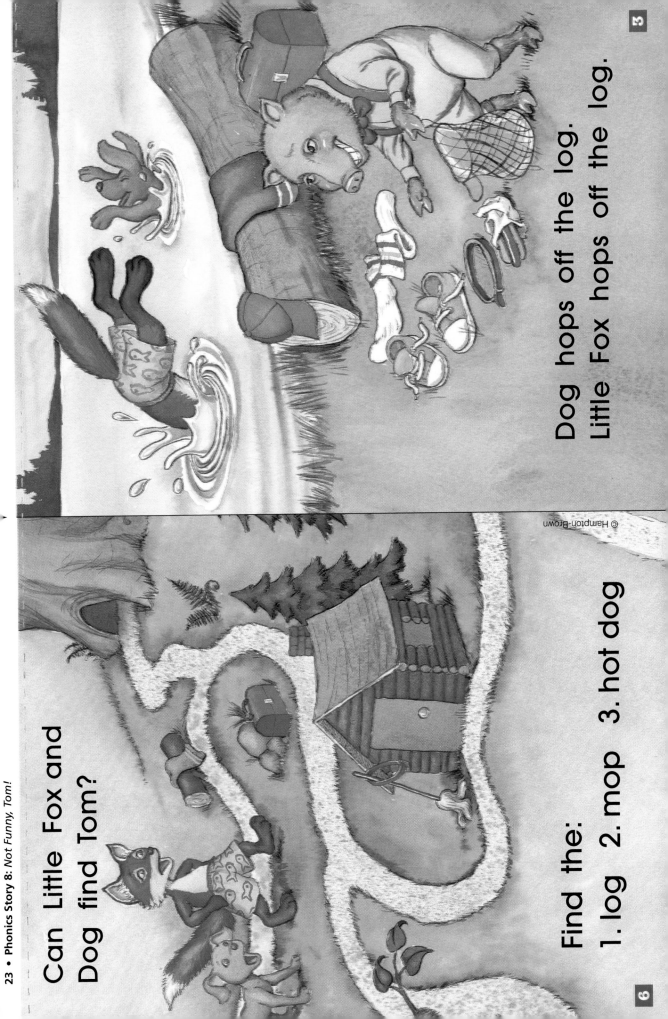

Can Little Fox and
Dog find Tom?

Find the:
1. log 2. mop 3. hot dog

Dog hops off the log.
Little Fox hops off the log.

3

6

Tom is very bad.

Tom takes the bag.

Zigzag Pig

Zigzag Pig did it!

Tom the pig is "It."

Tom puts in the pin.
Tom wins!

Tom zigs and hits a box.

3

You can do it, Tom!
You can win!

6

Tom zags and tips the jam.

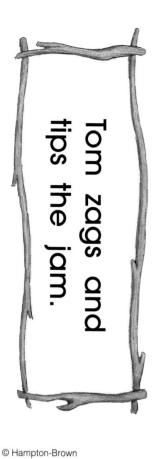

He zigzags into Little Fox.

Pup in the Mud

Pup jumps
in the tub!

Pup has a
lot of fun!

4

Pup yaps at the fox.
Pup bats the bug.
Pup jumps in the box.

Pup yaps at the cat.
Pup tips the jug.
Pup tugs on the rug.

Hidden Hens

Look for the hidden hens.
Find a hen in a jet.
Find a hen with a net.
Find a hen on an egg.

Find a hen on a peg.
Find a hen with a pen.
Find a hen with some men.

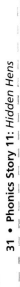

Count the Red Hens.
How many are there?
Count the hidden hens.
How many are there?

How many hens are there in all?

☐ + ☐ = ☐

The End

Tick Tock

"Quack, quack,"
said the duck.
"Get up, Pup.
You will miss the fun."

"Come up the hill.
Do not miss the fun!"

Peck, peck went the hen.
"Get up, Pup.
You will miss the fun."

3

© Hampton-Brown

"Quick, Pup, quick!"
his friends said.

6

Lick, lick went the kitten.
"Get up, Pup.
You will miss the fun."

Ring a ding went the bell!
That got Pup up!

Let's Go with Meg and Ben

Meg and Ben go to town. Let's go, too.

1. Get off the bus and go left.

2. Go to Nell's Plants.

3. Go to the Quick Stop.

4. Find Pet Pen. Where can it be?

5. Go past the flag to Hi-Ho Hot Dogs.

6. Oh, no! Meg is lost. Help Meg and
   Ben get back to the bus stop.

Meg and Ben go to town. They get off the bus and go to:

1. _____

2. _____

3. _____

4. _____

We went, too!

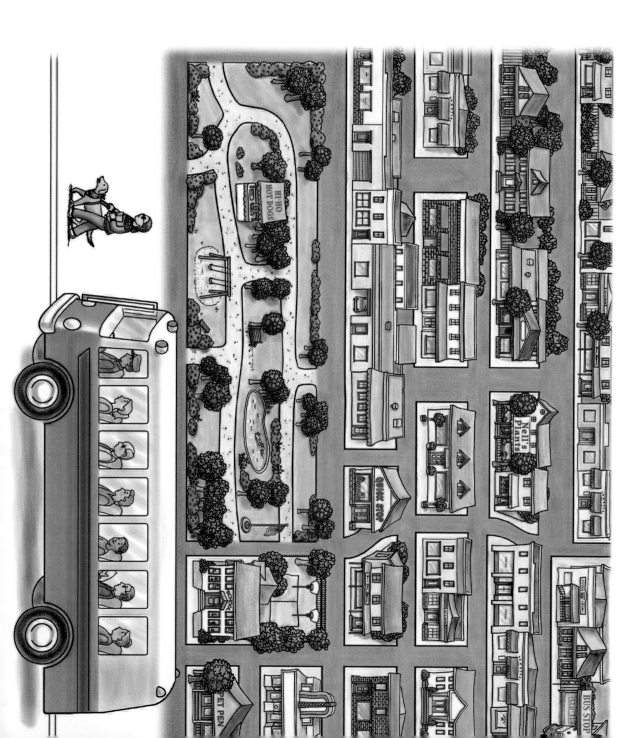

Name Game

Kate tells Mom the
name. "You are a cake!"

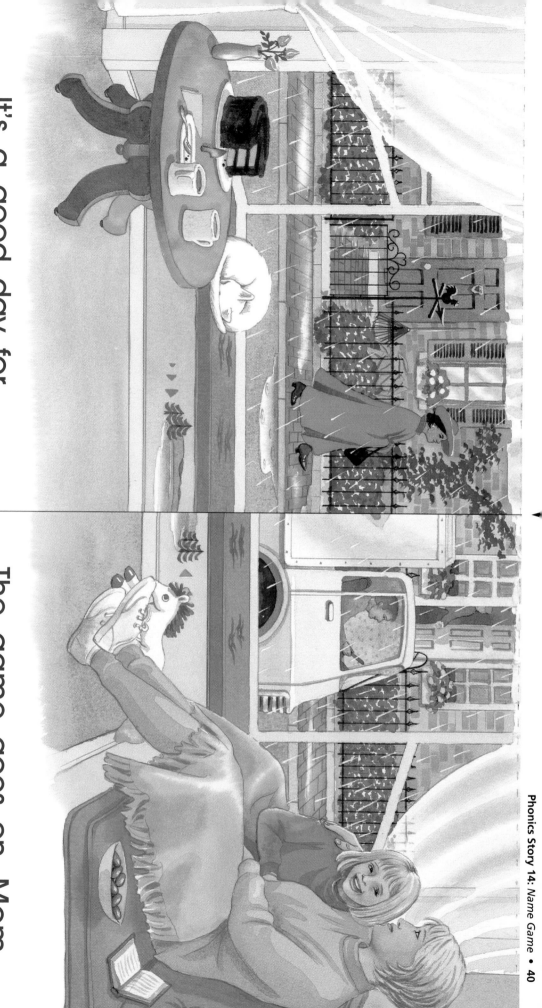

It's a good day for Mom and Kate to make up a game.

The game goes on. Mom tells Kate, "I am good. You bake me. Tell me my name."

Mom starts the game. She
tells Kate, "I am like a jacket.
I am red. Tell me my name."

3

Mom gets it. She tells
Kate, "You are a gate!"

6

Kate gets it. She tells Mom, "You are a cape!"

The game goes on. Kate tells Mom, "I let you in. I let you out. Tell me my name."

Jay in the Rain

In the little nest!

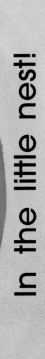

8

Jay goes on
her way. Where
will she lay
her eggs?

Jay has to
lay her eggs.
Where can she
go to get out
of the rain?

Jay goes to the
box of nails, but a
man yells at her.

6

Jay goes to
the mailbox, but
she can't get in.

4

Jay goes to the
pail, but the kids
say, "Go on!"

5

What more can you find?
Make a list.

A Rose
Is a Home

A bug is on the rose.
Find the bug.
A mole is in the hole.
Find the mole.

A pup is in Ray's home.
Find the pup.

Kate, Ray, and Joan find
"The Gold Toad." They give
Mr. Jones the map. He
gives them a lot of gold
for it!

The Gold Toad

Kate, Ray, and Joan
find an old map.
Kate picks it up.

At Low Dock, they
find more of the map.
It tells them to go to
"The Gold Toad."
"The Gold Toad."
"Let's go!" they say.

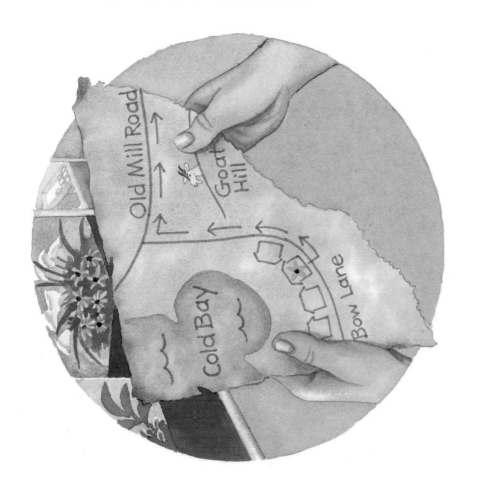

The friends look at the map. It tells them to go to Old Mill Road.

Joan finds a boat at the lake. The friends hop in and row the boat to Low Dock.

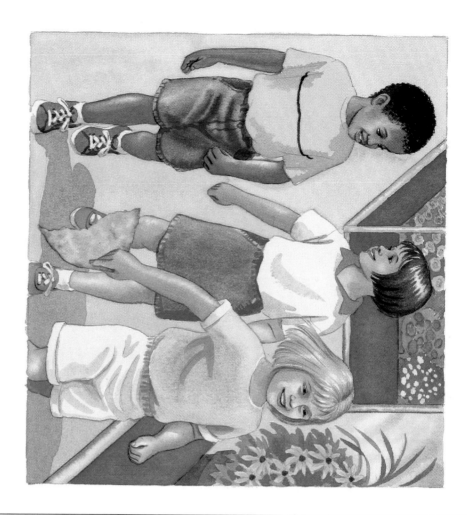

"Where is Old Mill Road?"
Ray and Joan say.
"Follow me," Kate tells them.

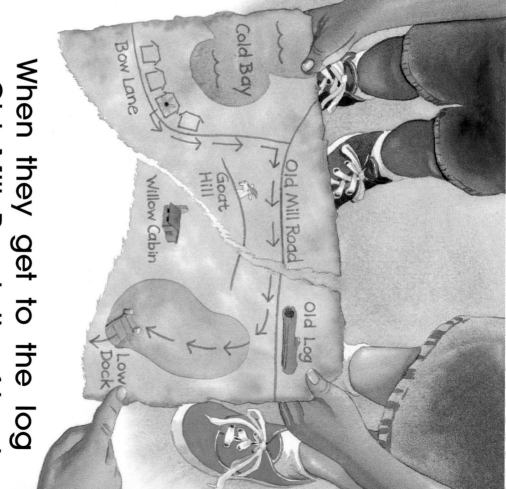

When they get to the log on Old Mill Road, the friends find more of the map. It tells them to go to Low Dock.

What a Ride!

"What a ride!" I said.
"Let's go one more time!"

My friend Mike and I went to Bay Rides. We got to go on the Dip and Dive.

At the end of the ride, the Dip and Dive fell a mile! It's a good thing I was by Mike's side.

The Dip and Dive went up, up, up, up, up, up. I said to Mike, "Get set for the ride of your life!"

The ride went by the:
1. bike 2. kite 3. five 4. nine

5. dime 6. pine 7. pipe

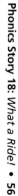

4

5

Nighttime Tale

A lad rose from the light. "You are good," he said. "You fed me when I was just a cat. I hope I am the one you will wed."

The End

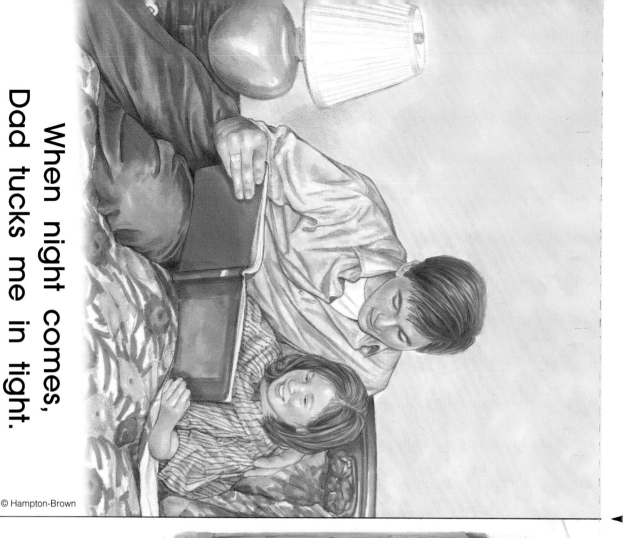

When night comes,
Dad tucks me in tight.

© Hampton-Brown

At sunrise, the maid went
to the well high on the hill.
When she got back, she saw
a fan of light on the rug.

He sits on my bed and
tells me a nighttime tale.

3

The cat ate the pie and
went right to bed. The milk
maid put out the light.

There was an old cat
who was all ribs and bones.
He was quite a sight!

One day he saw a milk
maid. He said with a sigh,
"Might I have a sip of milk?"
"You may have a bit of
milk and some pie, too," said
the maid. "Come in and lie
on the rug."

See It by the Sea

What did you see? Write some things.

_____

_____

_____

_____

_____

_____

4

See it leap out of the sea.
See its rays of heat.

See a fish in its beak.
See them on everyone's feet.
See it play in the seaweed.

See it eaten on a bun.
See it dive into the waves.
See what the seal sits upon.

One Foggy Night

It was the night of the comet...

As we got to the top, the comet lit up the sky. What a sight! The comet went right by us!

4

As the comet rose in the sky, the night got foggy. Becky said, "Come on, let's go up to the top of the hill."

We ran up the rocky hill. We got all muddy and messy, but that was all right.

THE END

Who Plays a Tune?

1. Mike plays a tune on a tub. Find him.

2. Becky plays a tune on a flute. Find her.

3. Duke the dog plays a tune. Find him.

4. A cow plays a tune with a bell. Find her.

5. A man in a blue suit plays a tune. Find him.

6. A cute mule plays a tune. Find her.

A BIG MESS

What a big mess!
A maple leaf is on the
rug, and a bugle is on
the bed. Mike needs
to pick up his stuff.
Can you help him?

Find the
✓ bugle
✓ puzzle
✓ maple leaf
✓ beetle
✓ apple
✓ Bubble Fun bottle

What did Mike pick up?

1. _____

2. _____

3. _____

4. _____

Everyone Goes to Sacks and Suits

Everyone goes up, up, and up. They go up to the top. They see lots of sights and lots of lights. And that's not all!

Everyone goes up.
They go up to 2.

A kid gets off to look
at the games, boats,
bikes, and dolls.

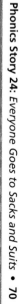

A man gets off to look at the suits, ties, jackets, coats, and hats.

3

Everyone goes up and up. They go up to 6.

6

Everyone goes up and up. They go up to 4.

A family gets off to look at the pots, pans, rugs, and mugs.

4

5

The Bud and Leaf

"And that's how the vine got so big," said Holly and her mom.

Holly and her
mom went to Miss
Hobb's to get some
seeds. They saw Miss
Hobb's rose vine.

"What a great vine,"
Holly said. "How did
it get so big?"

"Yes, and the roses
popped out!" said Miss Hobb.

The Bud and Leaf

"It all started,"
Miss Hobb said,
"when I planted
the vine and
the sun beamed
down."

3

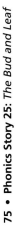

"You planted the vine,
the sun beamed down,
a bud poked out, and
the rain soaked the vine,
and you ripped out the
weeds?" said Holly.

10

"You planted the vine and the sun beamed down?" said Holly.

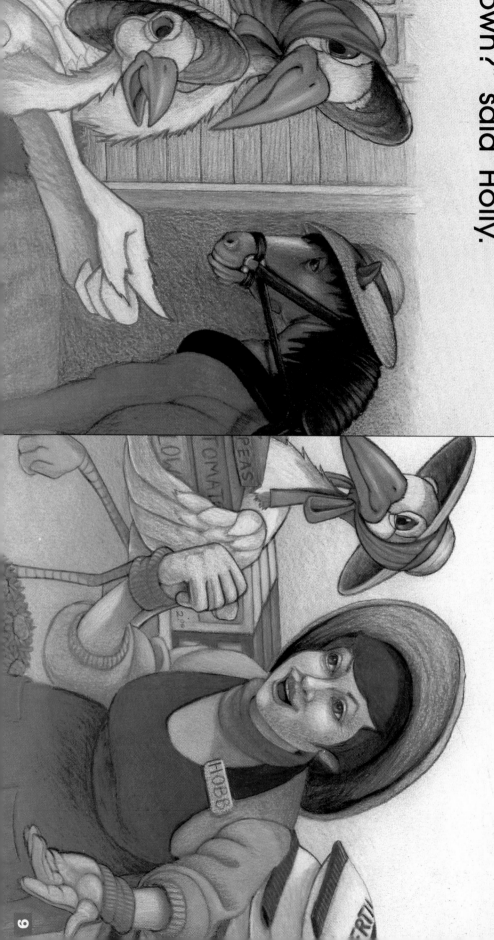

"Yes, and I ripped out the weeds," said Miss Hobb.

4

6

9

"You planted the vine, the sun beamed down, a bud poked out, and the rain soaked the vine?" said Holly.

"Yes, and a bud poked out!" said Miss Hobb.

© Hampton-Brown

5

8

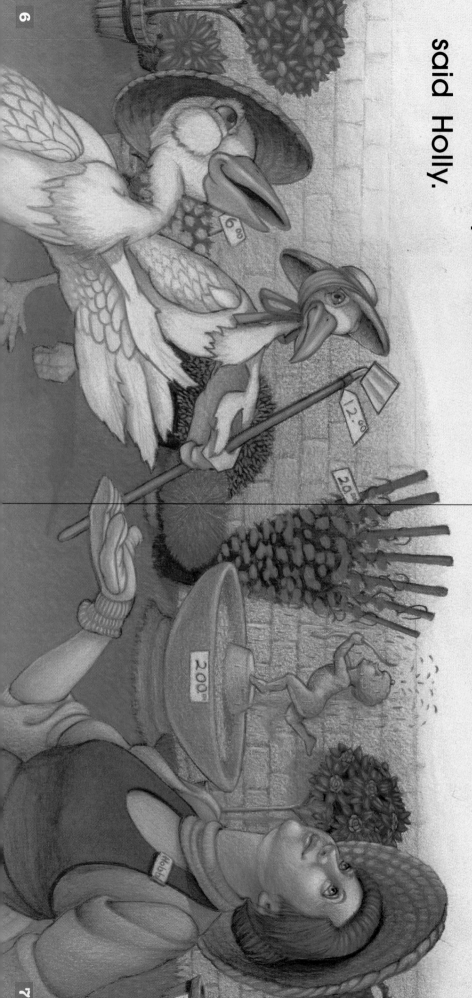

"You planted the vine,
the sun ☀ beamed down,
and a bud 🌱 poked out?"
said Holly.

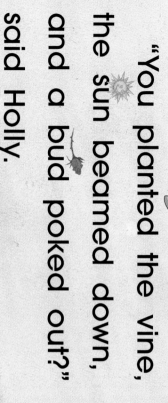

"Yes, and the rain soaked
the vine," said Miss Hobb.

Tusks and Tails

Who looked up? Draw each animal's face.

1.	**2.**
3.	**4.**

4

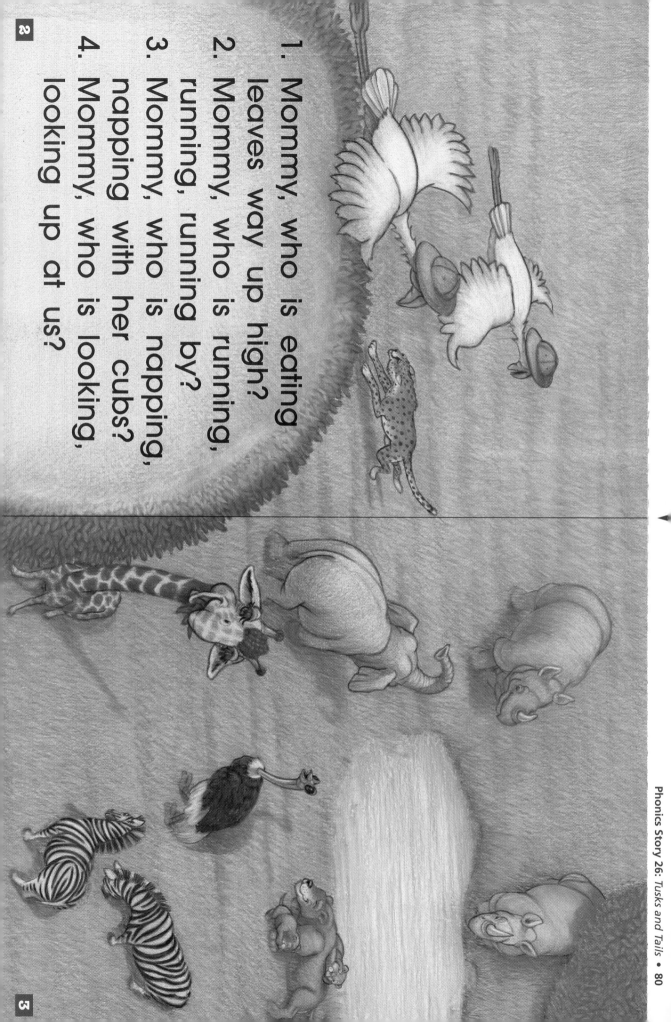

1. Mommy, who is eating
   leaves way up high?
2. Mommy, who is running,
   running, running by?
3. Mommy, who is napping,
   napping with her cubs?
4. Mommy, who is looking,
   looking up at us?

Up the Slope

"I bet you can't get your sled to the top," yells Clay. "I bet I can," yells Flame.

1. Flame tugs his sled up to the blue cap, but slips back to the fluffy bunny.

2. Flame tugs his sled up to the black cave, but slips back to the blanket.

3. Flame tugs his sled up to the flat rock and gets to the top.

Show how Flame got to the top. Draw a line.

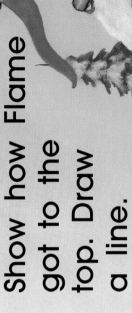

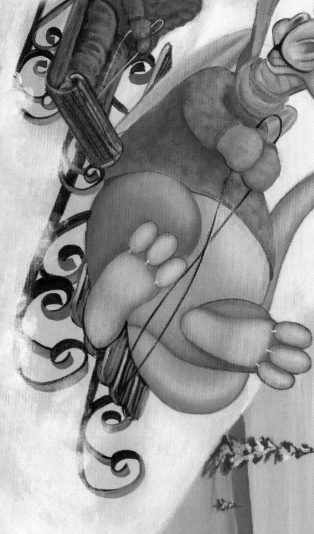

Clay and Flame fly down
the slope!
"I bet you can't beat me
to the bottom," yells Flame.
"I bet I can," yells Clay.

Flame's Dream

Flame woke up. "Oh!"
he cried. "What a treat! My
dream has come true!"
The kids laughed and
said, "Yes, this is our
treat for you!"

8

Flame liked kids. When kids came down the trail, he always gave them treats.

Flame began to dream of sky and sun. The kids mixed the paint. Flame dreamed of rainbows. The kids painted and painted.

He gave them little drums,
and he gave them rides on
his long, green tail.

3

Flame went to sleep,
but the kids did not leave.
They said, "Let's give Flame
a treat!" The kids got pots
of paint.

6

One rainy day, Flame was not on the trail when the kids came by. So they went to his cave. Flame was in bed!

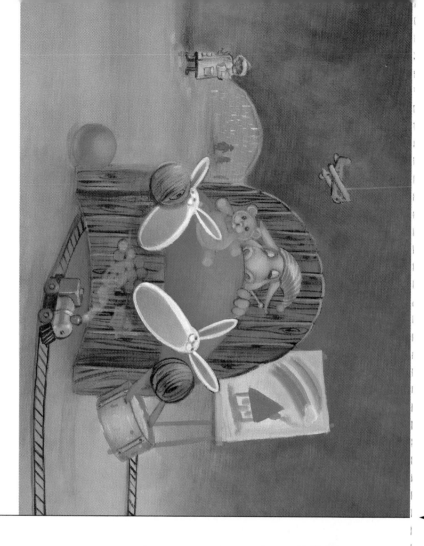

"I'm too sick to play," he groaned. "The day is too gray to get out of bed."

"That's all right," said the kids. "Go to sleep. We will come back."

4

5

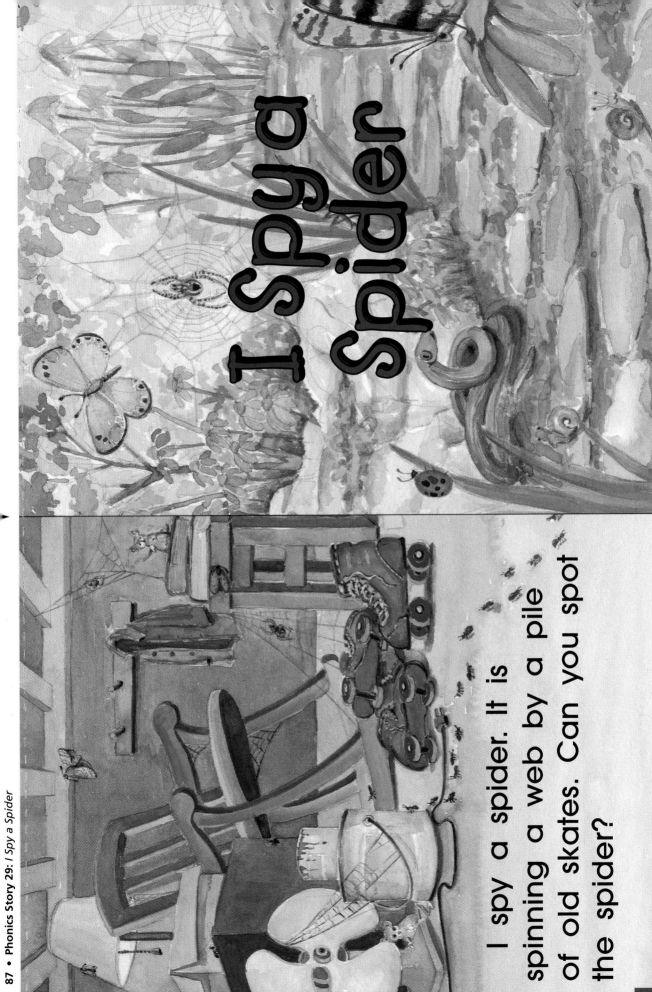

I Spy a Spider

I spy a spider. It is spinning a web by a pile of old skates. Can you spot the spider?

4

2

I spy a spider. It is spinning a web by a skunk. Can you spot the spider?

3

I spy a spider. It is spinning a web on the stem of a rose. Can you spot the spider?

How the Evening Star Got in the Sky

It landed high in the sky
and hung there like a
bright light.
And that is how the
evening star got in the sky.

8

Skunk saw a bright stone
at the bottom of the lake.
He bent down to get it.

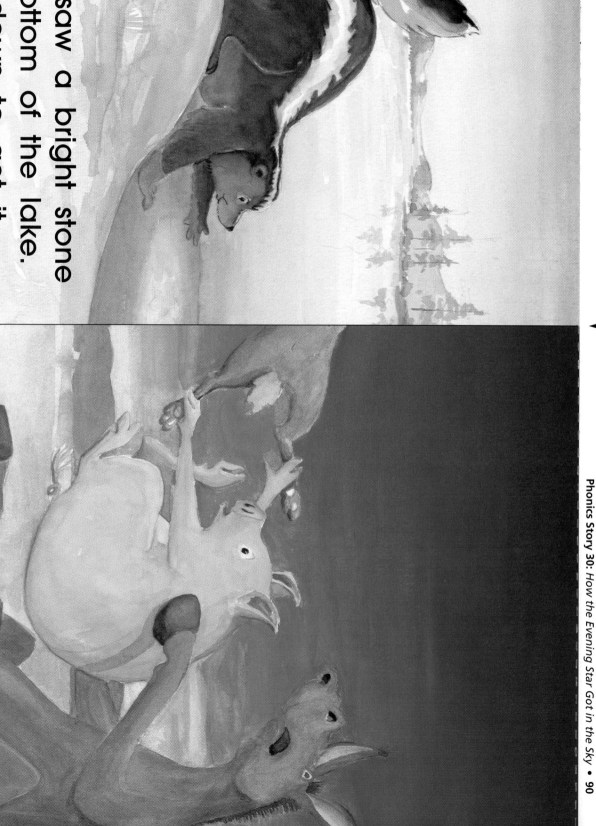

Rabbit came by to get a drink. "Lend me a hand," said Skunk. "See that bright stone at the bottom of the lake. I want to get it."

3

So Mule hung onto Pig. When Skunk grabbed the stone, Mule yanked everyone up, but...z-z-zing! The stone went flying out of Skunk's hand.

6

So Rabbit hung onto Skunk. Pig came by to get a drink. "Lend us a hand," said Rabbit. "See that bright stone at the bottom of the lake. We want to get it."

4

So Pig hung onto Rabbit. Mule came by to get a drink. "Lend us a hand," said Pig. "See that bright stone at the bottom of the lake. We want to get it."

5

LOOK PAST THE GATE

© Hampton-Brown

Look past the gate.
Look for the stump.
Look for Snake hiding
from his friend Skunk.

4

Look past the gate.
Look left and right.
Look for things that are
out of sight.

2

Look for a nest and a vest.
Look for a lamp.
Look for a raft and a gift.
Look for a stamp.

3

The Animal Game

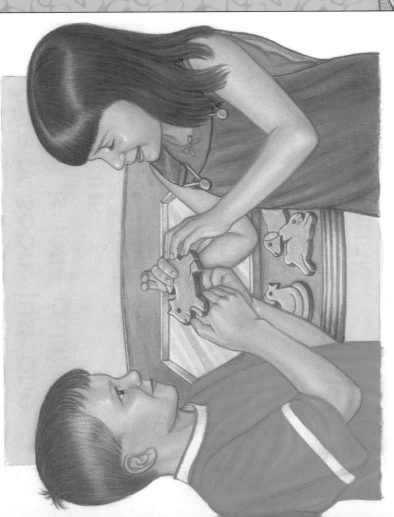

What will Chela and Chuck do?

How to Play

- Listen to clues about an animal.

- If you name the right animal, you get to take it.

Pretty soon, just one animal is left—a little chipmunk.

"It's mine!" says Chela.

"No, it's mine!" says Chuck.

They each reach for the chipmunk.

Chuck and Chela made a batch of animal cookies.

Chela starts. She says, "I chase cats. Who am I?"

Chuck knows. What animal does he take?

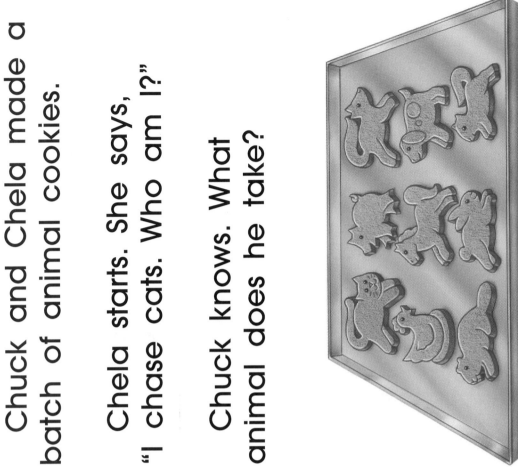

Chela and Chuck each get a lot of animals!

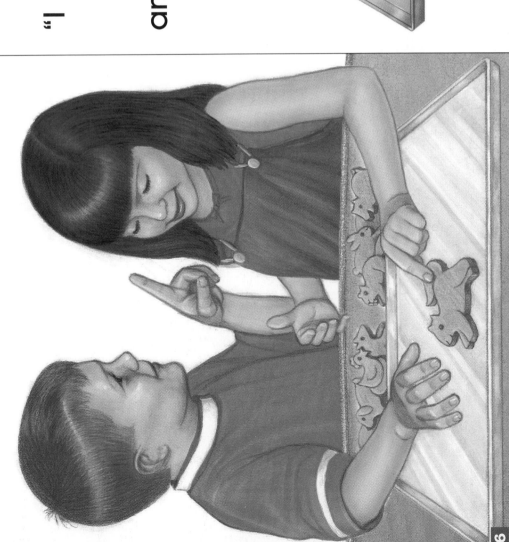

Chuck says, "I chop down trees to make dams. Who am I?"

Chela knows. What animal does she take?

Then Chela says, "I have a beak and wings. My baby is a chick. Who am I?"

Chuck knows. What animal does he take?

TEETH AND TAIL

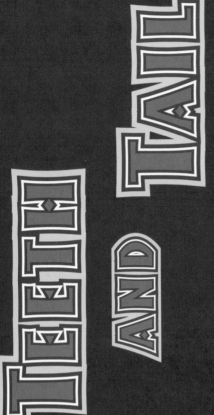

Chela laughs. "It must be! Everyone made the same thing!"

8

Chela is making a great costume. She starts with some green cloth to make the suit.

She bangs on Beth's door. Thump! Thump! Thump!

"What a great costume!" says Beth.

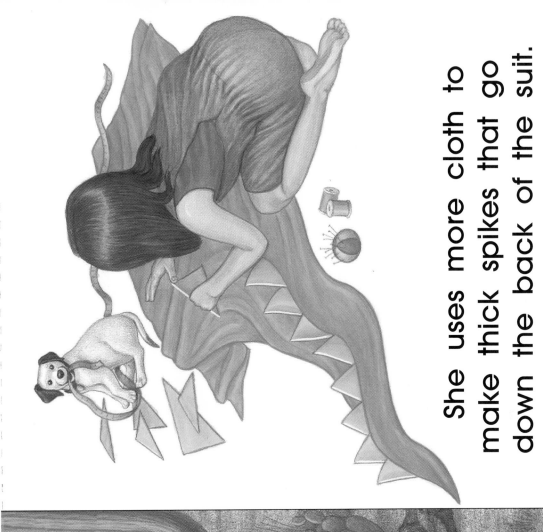

She uses more cloth to make thick spikes that go down the back of the suit.

Chela goes down the path on her way to Beth's. Thud! Thud! What a sight she makes! Chela thinks, "I'm going to scare everyone to bits!"

4

She makes long spikes
for the end of the tail.
She thinks the spikes look
pretty scary!

She puts thick
pads on the
bottom of
the feet.

She finds some
rickrack trim that
will make great
teeth.

5

Shadow Shapes

Cactus plants make great shadow shapes. Chela makes more shapes with rocks and sticks. Find the shadows that look like a:

1. ship
2. fish
3. shed
4. shell
5. sheep

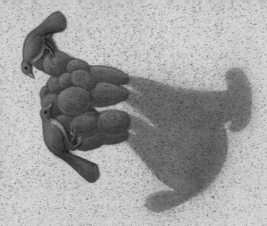
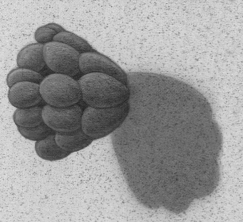
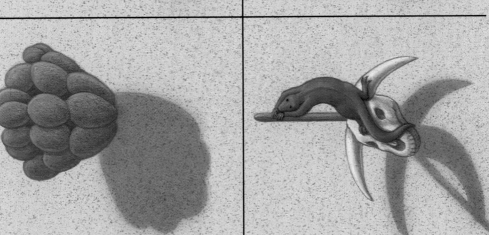
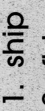

Draw what made this shadow.

Chela
and the
Whale

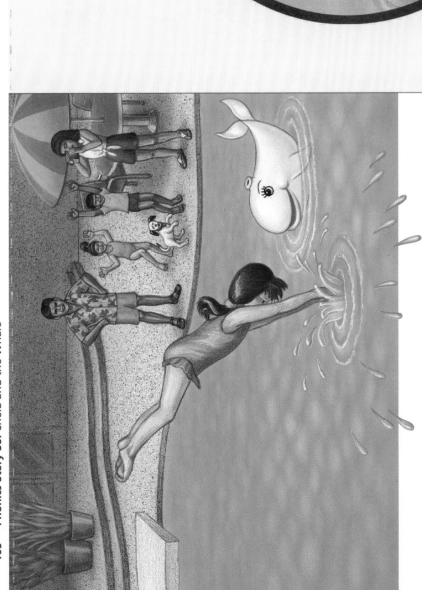

Chela dove in and grabbed her little white whale. What fun they had while everyone laughed and clapped!

"Come on, Chela," Dad said. "Dive in!"

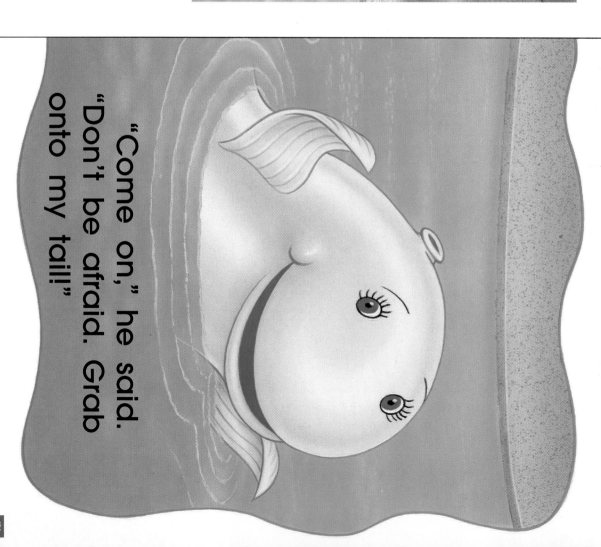

"Come on," he said. "Don't be afraid. Grab onto my tail!"

7

Chela sat while everyone waited. Soon she started to daydream. She dreamed that her little white whale was talking to her.

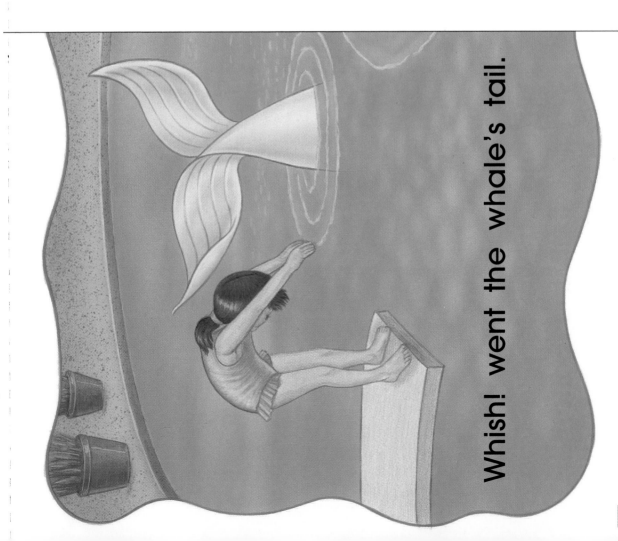

Whish! went the whale's tail.

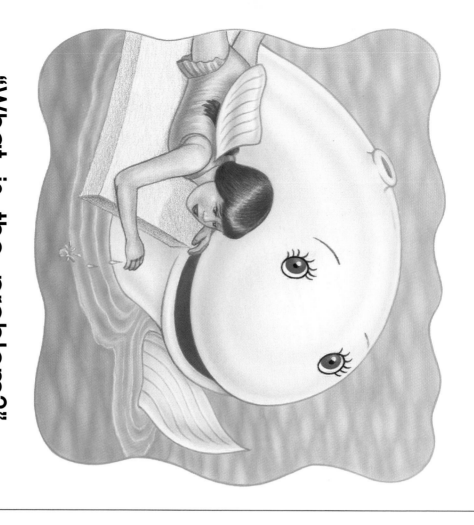

"What is the problem?"
the whale said. "Why don't
you dive in?"

4

"I'm afraid," Chela said.
"I'm not a whale like you.
What if I hit the bottom
when I dive in?"

5

Carl Wins a Prize

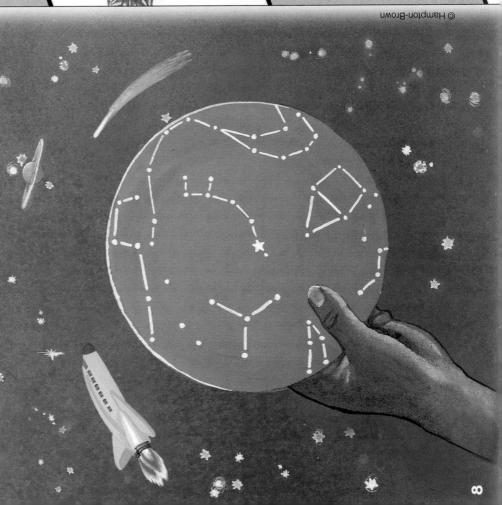

8

In the *Ferndale Times*,
Carl saw a puzzle contest
for kids.

Seeing Stars

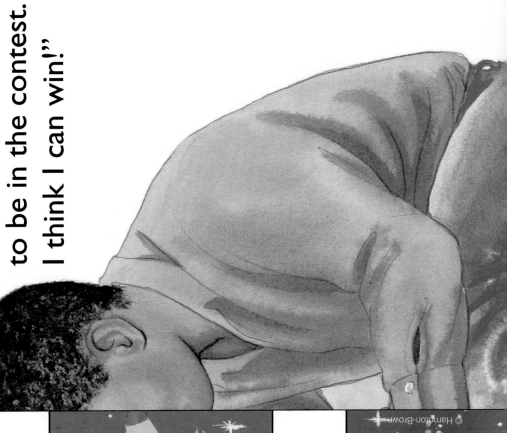

Now you can do the puzzle, too. Have fun!

Across

1 We will fly to the stars in a s t _ s h _ _.

2 It's fun to find stars on a star c h _ _ _.

4 We see starlight in the d _ _ _.

5 The North S _ _ _ is easy to find.

Down

3 Look for stars from your b _ _ _ y _ _ _.

6 The stars s p _ _ _ _ and shine.

© Hampton-Brown

6

Carl said to his dad, "I'm really good at doing puzzles. I want to be in the contest. I think I can win!"

3

Carl did the puzzle. It was all about stars. Many girls and boys sent in puzzles, but Carl won!

His picture was in the *Ferndale Times*.

Ferndale Times

Star Wizard Wins Puzzle Contest

Carl Martin likes puzzles. "I do them morning and night!" he says.

Tomorrow: a report on Ferndale's Special Day

FERNDALE'S SPECIAL DAY

This is a special day in Ferndale. Boys and girls are marching down Ferndale Road.

Ms. Stern stands on the corner and takes pictures of:

1. Robert and his red bird

2. Hector in his furry hat

3. Carla in her purple dress

4. Shirleen with her curls and bows

5. Herman in a shirt with the number 13

Can you find them, too?

Ms. Stern prints her story in the *Ferndale Times*.

Which of these goes under each picture?

1. Carla and Shirleen hurry down the road together.

2. Hector is hot in his furry hat.

3. Robert's little friend says, "Pretty bird!"

4. Herman turns and waves to his family.

Ferndale Times

Ferndale's Special Day!

Ferndale's
Baby Deer

© Hampton-Brown

Look what happened in Ferndale!

Ferndale Times

Baby Deer Lost in Park

A lost baby deer showed up in Dairymill Park last night. John Reardon tried to steer the deer to a safe clearing in the park, but the deer ran off into the...

If anyone sees the baby deer, call the Animal Rescue Team. Do not try to rescue the deer yourself.

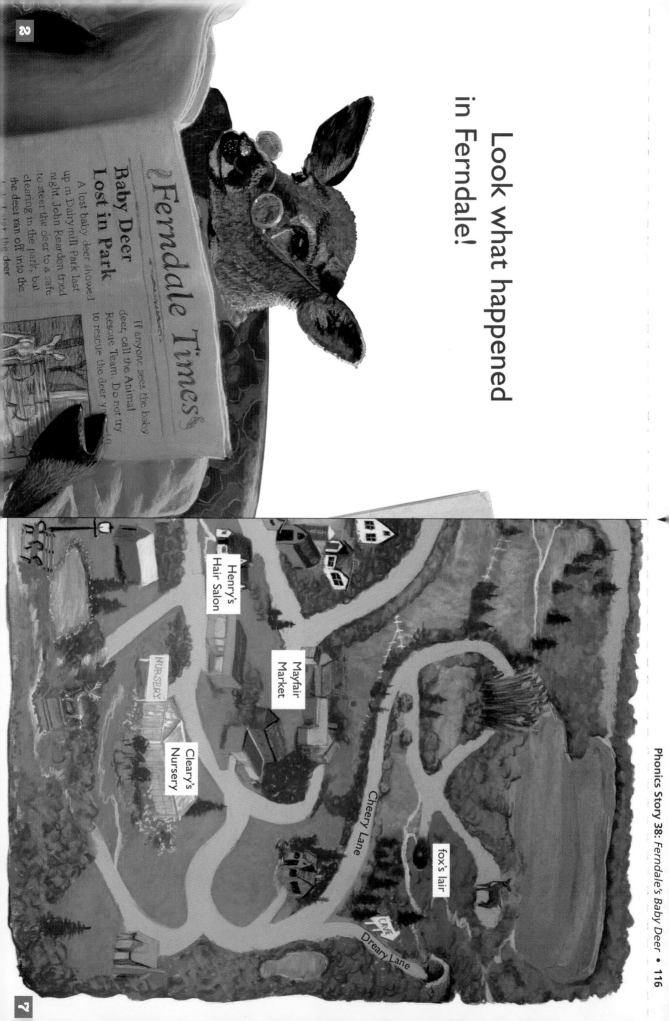

Henry's Hair Salon

Mayfair Market

NURSERY

Cleary's Nursery

Cheery Lane

fox's lair

CAVE

Dreary Lane

Steer the baby deer down the path to the forest. Go to:

1. Earrings and Things
2. Henry's Hair Salon
3. Cleary's Nursery
4. Cherry Lane
5. past the fox's lair and home

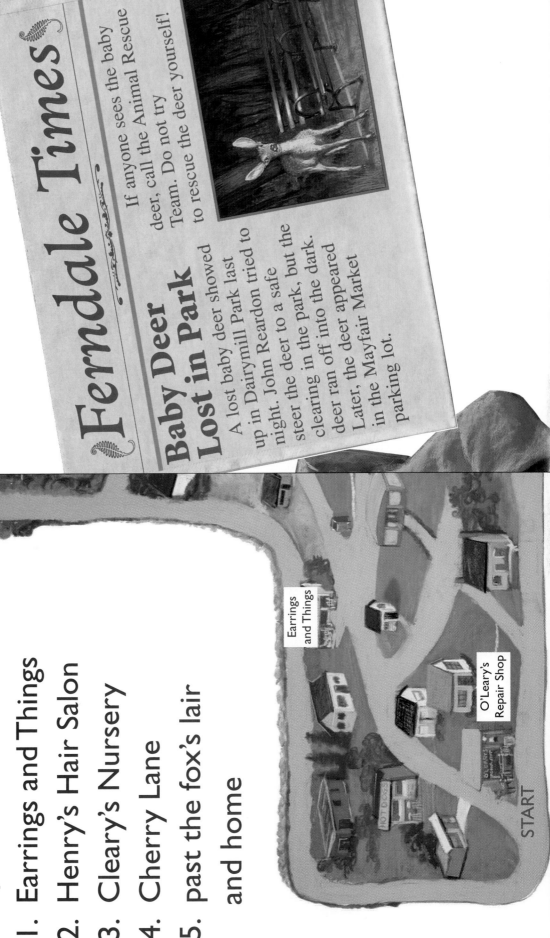

START

Earrings and Things

O'Leary's Repair Shop

Ferndale Times

Baby Deer Lost in Park

A lost baby deer showed up in Dairymill Park last night. John Reardon tried to steer the deer to a safe clearing in the park, but the deer ran off into the dark. Later, the deer appeared in the Mayfair Market parking lot.

If anyone sees the baby deer, call the Animal Rescue Team. Do not try to rescue the deer yourself!

4

The baby deer is still far from its home in the forest.

The mama deer is waiting for it to return.

Can you help the baby deer get back home? Turn the page and try.

5

How Many Beetles?

8

Living things are hidden here.
How many can you see?

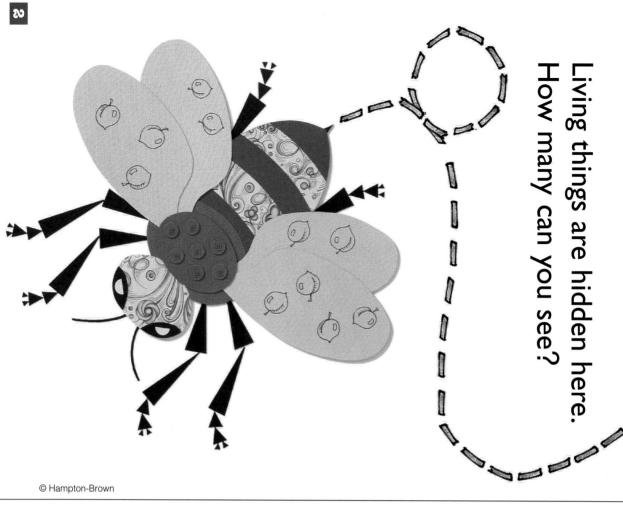

How many dragonflies
are in the cricket?
How many crickets
are going by?

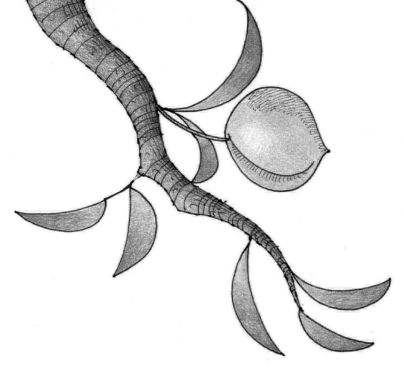

One little peach hangs on
a branch. How many
peaches are in the bee?

One little roach is there
by the stone.
How many roaches are
in the dragonfly?

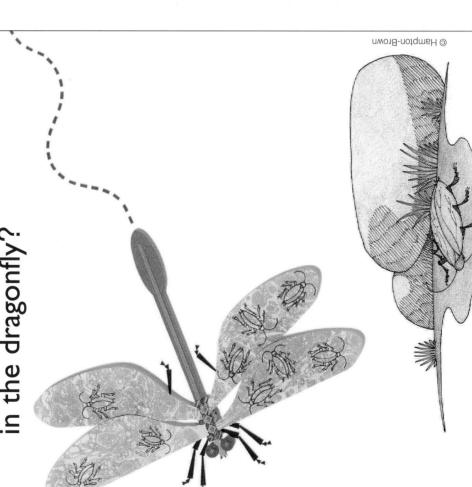

One little bee
goes buzzing by.
How many bees
are in the butterfly?

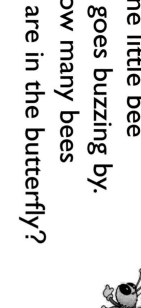

How many butterflies
are in the beetle?
How many beetles
do you spy?

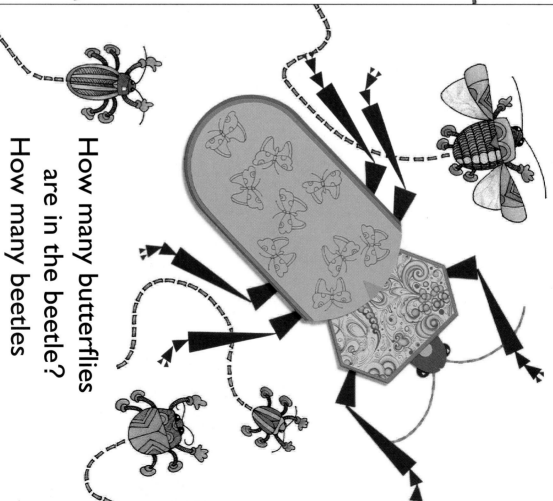

4

5

Night of the Full Moon

The first people who
lived in the West were fine
storytellers, and they still are.
Sometimes a storyteller
made pictures in the sand
and used them to tell a story.

Do you know what story
these sand pictures tell?

moon   raccoon   stool   roof

rope   eagle   spoon

Turn the page and find out.

2

Use the sand pictures to write your own story.

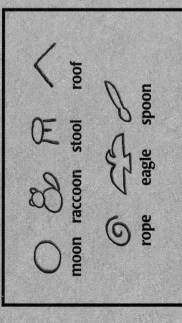

moon   raccoon   stool   roof

rope   eagle   spoon

3

10

Raccoon's Moon

Long ago, in the Before Time, the ◯ hung like a bowl of milk in the sky. ℬ said, "I want to taste the creamy milk that fills the ◯."

So ℬ got up on a ⋔, but he could not reach the ◯.

4

Now, some people say that Raccoon visits the moon when it is big. They say the moon gets smaller because Raccoon drinks its milk.

Do you think this is true? Eagle will tell you that it is.

9

The next night, he got up on a ⋀ , but he still couldn't reach the ○ . ⌁ flew by. He saw that ⅋ was feeling gloomy. ⅋ told him how much he wanted to taste the milk that fills the ○ . "All I need to do is reach it," he said.

"Grab that ⊚ ," cried ⌁ . "Throw me one end."

© Hampton-Brown

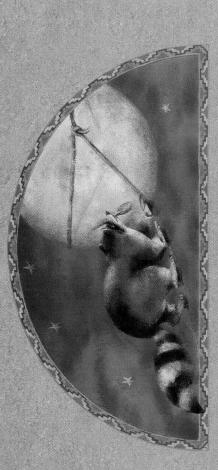

So ⅋ got a big ⌒ .
Then he grabbed the rope and started to climb.

At last he reached the ○ that hung like a bowl of milk in the sky.

⅋ sipped the sweet milk day after day. Soon the ○ began to grow smaller and smaller.

6

 held the  in his beak and flew to the  . He tied the  around the  . Then, after a long time,  saw  coming back.

7

"Go on, now," said  .

"The  is new and strong. It will hold you."

"What should I take with me?" asked  .

"Take a  ," said  .

"That is all you will need."

8

A Time Trip to

Auburn, U.S.A.

In years to come,
people will have
more things to
make life easier or
more fun. If you
go to Auburn in
the year 2069, you
will see all sorts of
new things.

3. A robot mows the [ ].

4. A robot hangs up
   the [ ].

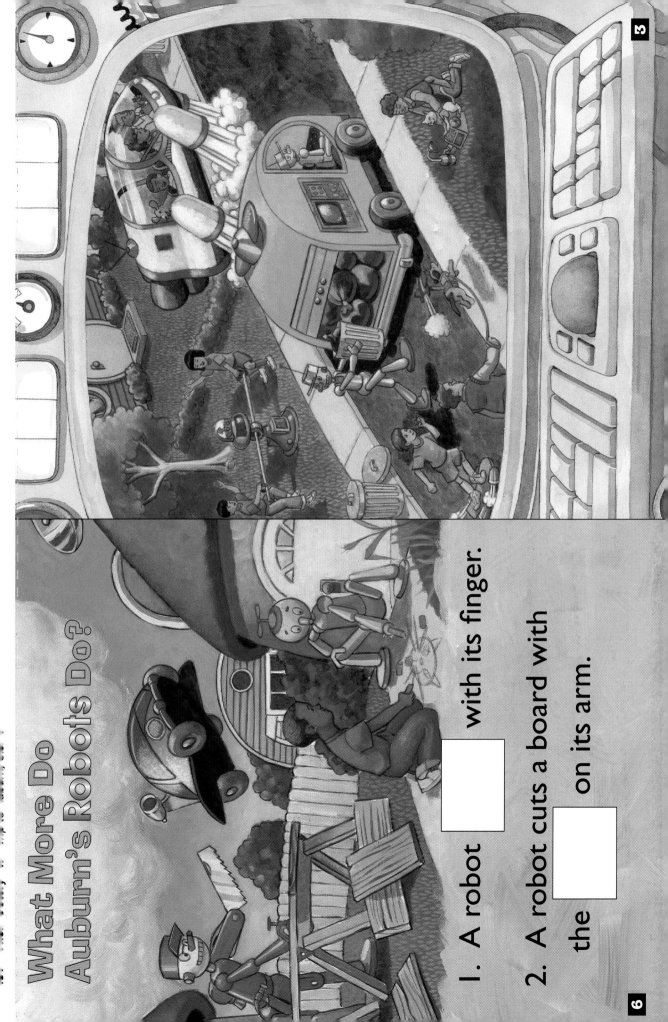

What More Do Auburn's Robots Do?

1. A robot [ ] with its finger.

2. A robot cuts a board with the [ ] on its arm.

4

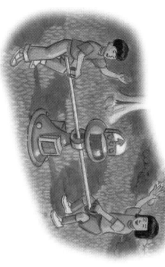

Kids get to play on automatic seesaws.

People have a better way to clean muddy paws.

People go places in rockets.
3 - 2 - 1 - Launch!

Robots pick up and haul trash.

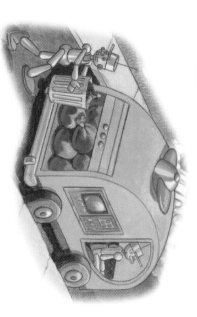

5

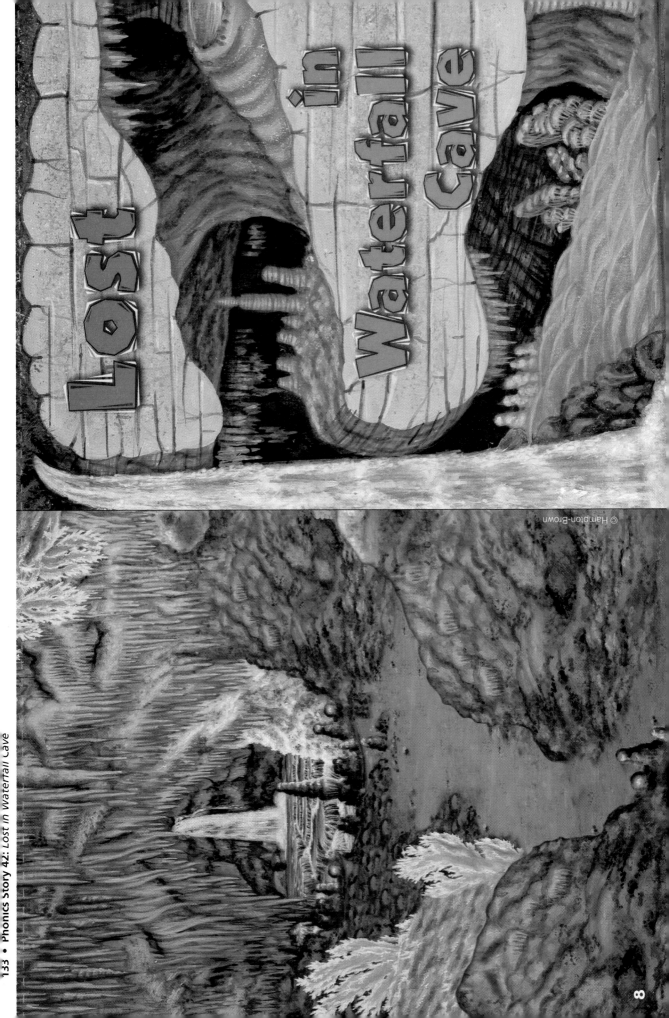

Lost in Waterfall Cave

8

A great waterfall made this cave. Almost all caves like this have deep, hidden places that look like fairylands.

Some of the rooms are quite tall. Stone forms hang from the top wall and also rise up from the bottom of the cave.

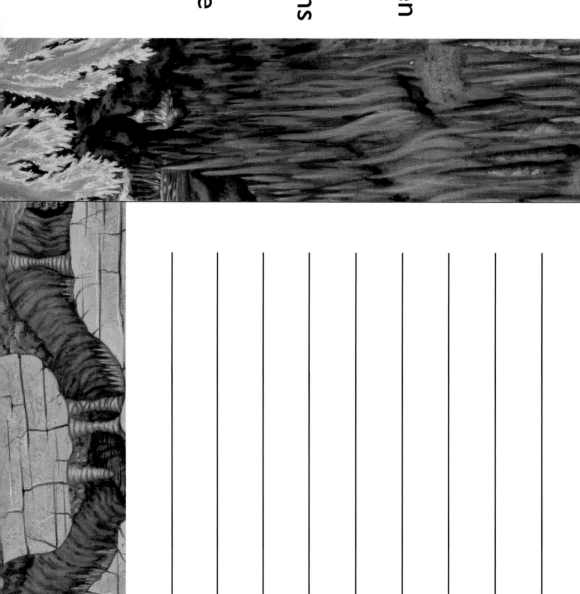

Pretend that you really are lost in a Waterfall Cave. Write a story. Tell how you got out.

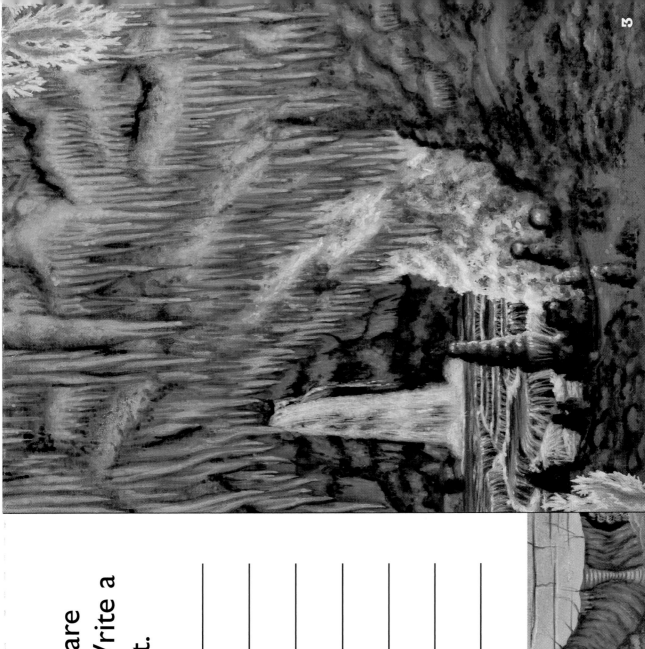

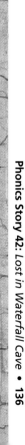

LOST!

YOU ARE HERE

You are lost in Waterfall Cave, but there is a way out. Find the stone forms that look like these things. Go past them and out of the cave.

1. the ball
2. the tree
3. the tall candle
4. the small pool
5. the salt shaker
6. the walnut

© Hampton-Brown

4

5

Paul likes his new book, and it looks like he is ready to go on a trip. Tell him good-by!

4

Ms. Brooks delivers the mail on foot in Anyplace, U.S.A. Yesterday she took this mail without backtracking:

• some hooks for Mr. Fisher
• a box of cookies for little Jerry
• a letter for Mrs. Wood
• a new book for Paul Cook

How did she go?

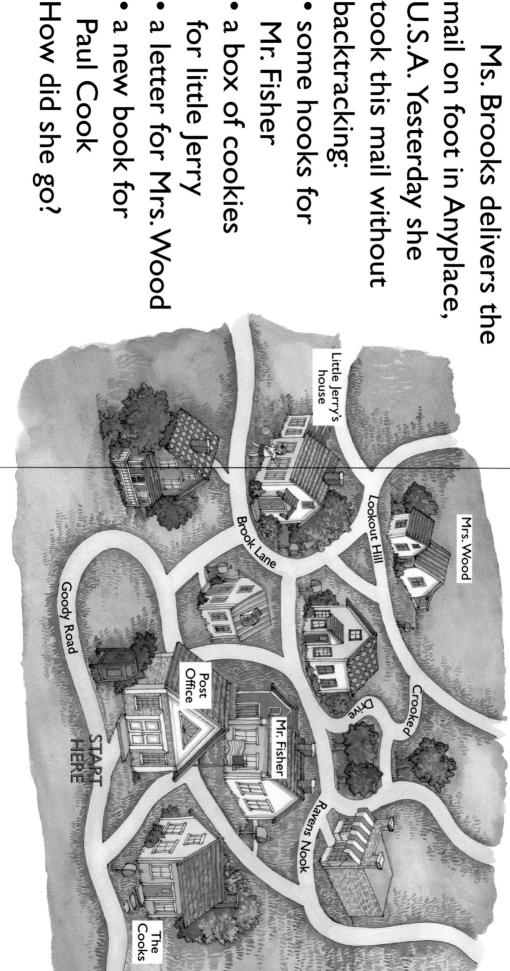

Little Jerry's house

Mrs. Wood

Brook Lane

Lookout Hill

Crooked Drive

Goody Road

Post Office

START HERE

Mr. Fisher

Ravens Nook

The Cooks

2

3

The Case of the Careless Princess

The Problem:

The princess has lost her cape... and cuff... and ring...

© Hampton-Brown

Where will her cat find Priscilla's cape and cuff and ring? Look again. You will find other things she has lost, too.

4

Once there was a princess who lived in an ice palace. Princess Priscilla lost things, not once, not twice, but all the time!

Nearly every day, she had to call on her cat to help her find what she had lost.

Lost: one cape
Last seen: last night

The princess is certain.

Lost: one lace cuff
Last seen: when she went out

Lost: one ring, a ruby set in a circle of gold
Last seen: this morning at the table

cape

cuff

ring

The Case of the Ginger Cookie Boy

The Problem:
Mrs. Good's ginger cookie boy is missing...

My cat followed the footprints and gumdrops. The ginger cookie boy hopped out the window and ran away through the garden all by himself.

CASE CLOSED!

Not the gentle
gentleman. He
was making
magic on stage.

Here's how Mrs. Good's
cat cracked the case...

Mrs. Good baked a nice ginger cookie boy with gumdrop buttons on his shirt.

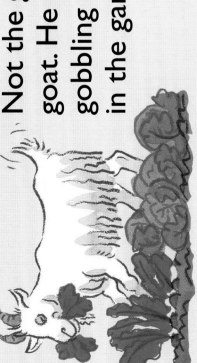

When she was ready for tea, the ginger cookie boy was gone. Mrs. Good asked her cat to help.

3

Who did it?

Not the giraffe. She was running in the yard.

Not the gabby goat. He was gobbling greens in the garden.

6

4

Who took Mrs. Good's ginger cookie boy?

5

Was it the giraffe?
Was it the gabby goat?
Was it the gentle gentleman?

The Case of Troy's Code

The Problem:
Cracking Troy's
Cookbook Code

145 • Phonics Story 46: The Case of Troy's Code

Code Key:

ABC	DEF	GHI	JKL
MNO	PQR	STU	VWX
			YZ

Write a message to a friend.
Use the code.

_____

_____

_____

_____

_____

_____

© Hampton-Brown

8

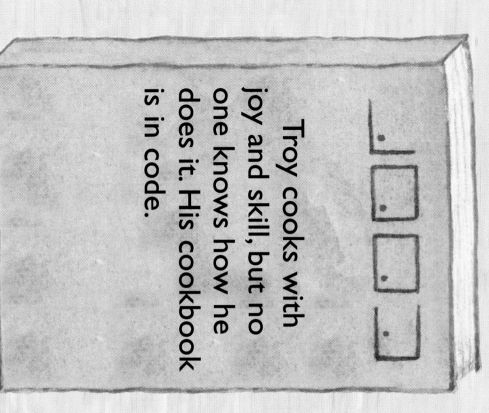

Troy cooks with joy and skill, but no one knows how he does it. His cookbook is in code.

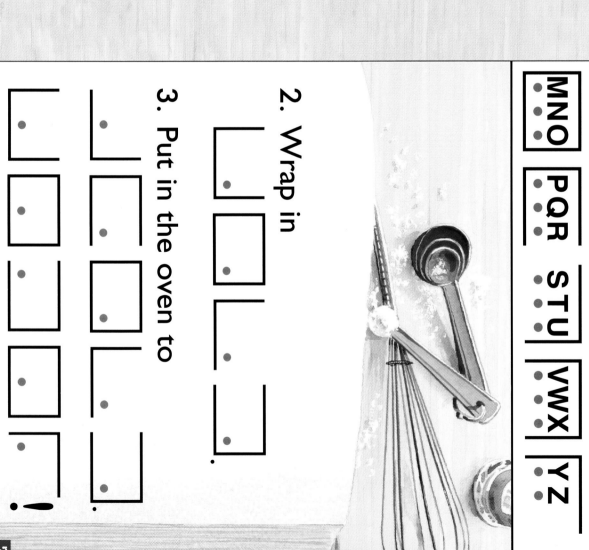

MNO	PQR	STU	VWX	YZ

2. Wrap in ☐ ☐ ☐ .

3. Put in the oven to ☐ ☐ ☐ . ☐ ☐ ☐ ☐ !

3

Code Key:

ABC	DEF	GHI	JKL
● ● ●	● ● ●	● ● ●	● ● ●

Now crack the code to find out how to cook Pork a la Troy.

PORK a la TROY

1. Moisten the pork ▢ ▢ ▢ with ▢ sauce.

6

Code Key:

ABC	DEF	GHI	JKL	MNO	PQR	STU	VWX	YZ

This is Troy's code:

Here is how I cracked it.

1. I looked at the first box. I found the matching box in the Code Key.

STU

2. Then I got the letter for the dot.

STU

That's how I knew that the first letter of the word is **S**. What are the rest of the letters?

S

Now join the letters. What does the code say?

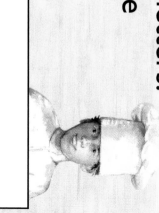

4

5

A Case for Hink-Pink Hound

The Problem:
Hink-Pink has lost his best bone.

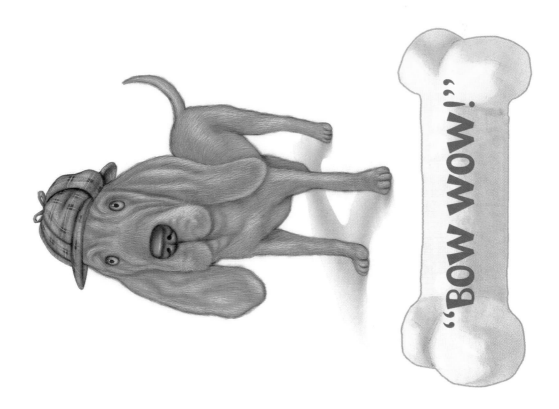

"BOW WOW!"

My pal Cal has a very smart hound. He is not just a sniffing hound. He is a sound hound.

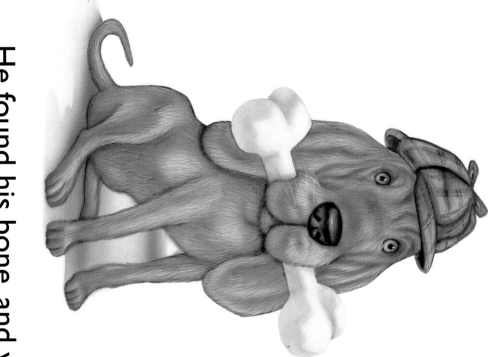

He found his bone, and you helped! Here's how Hink-Pink Hound says thank you...

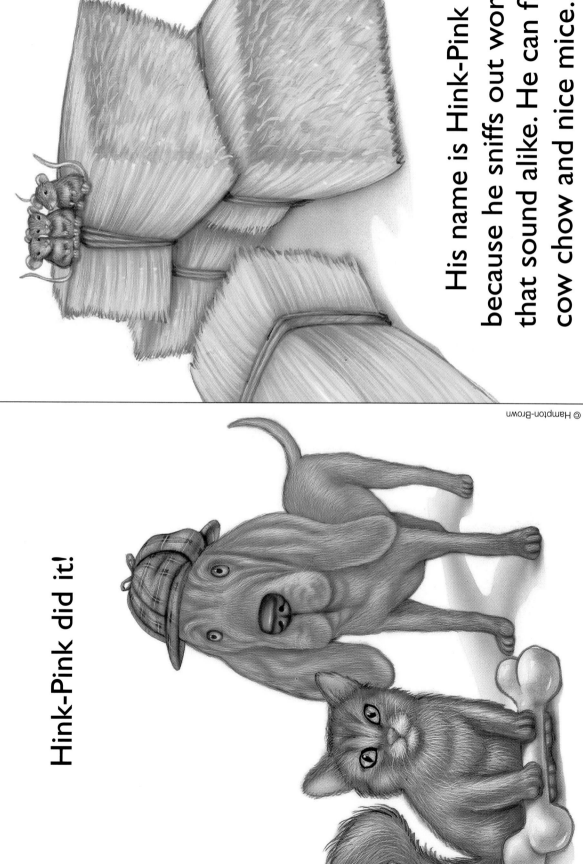

His name is Hink-Pink because he sniffs out words that sound alike. He can find cow chow and nice mice.

Hink-Pink did it!

Someone stole
Hink-Pink's bone.
He can find it if he
takes the right path.
Can you help him?

Find a
1. group that makes
   a lot of noise
2. tall house made
   of roses
3. home for a very
   small animal
4. father who is
   not happy
5. very large
   house pet

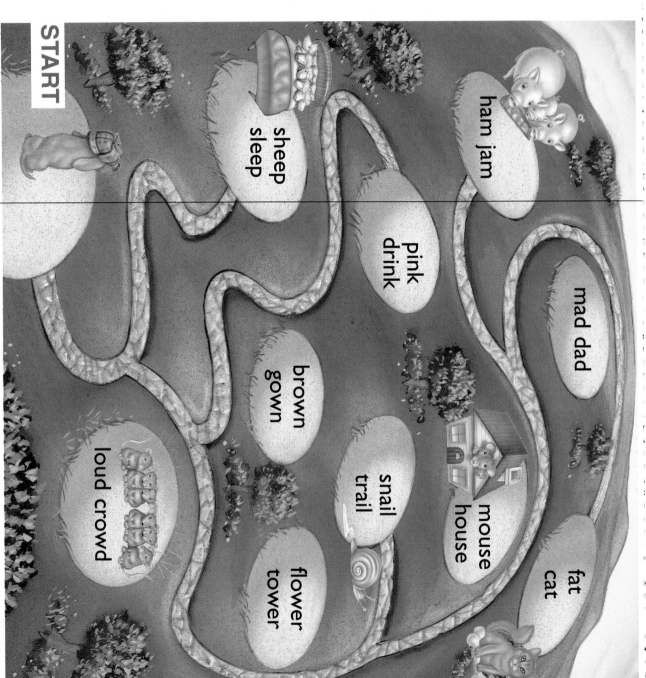

START

ham jam

sheep
sleep

pink
drink

mad dad

brown
gown

snail
trail

mouse
house

flower
tower

loud crowd

fat
cat

LOOK FOR A STAR

THE BRIGHTEST ROCK!

8

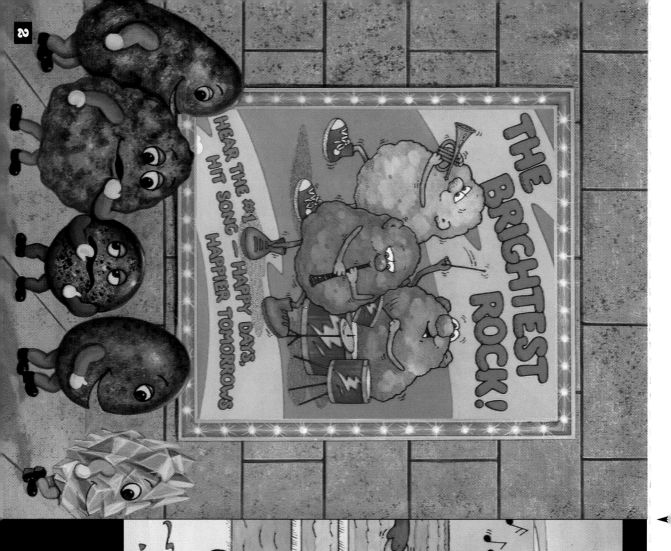

THE BRIGHTEST ROCK!

HEAR THE #1 HIT SONG — HAPPY DAYS, HAPPIER TOMORROWS

They sang "Happy Days, Happier Tomorrows." Everyone loved it!

Shining brighter,
Feeling lighter,
And our wedding
bells will chime,
Bringing happier
tomorrows 'til the
very end of time!

Making a hit film is one of the hardest jobs on earth. The film must tell a good story.

It has to have great music, greater sound effects, and the greatest special effects ever.

A hit film must have fine actors. That's why filmmakers want only the brightest stars to be in their films.

Under sunniest,
Under starriest,
Under bluest of
blue skies.
We'll have happy
days together,
Sharing joy that
never dies.

Ruby Stone got the part. She sang and danced with Granite Hill.

Four talented starlets tried out for a part in *The Brightest Rock!* The director wanted someone who had:

1. hair redder than a sunset
2. eyes bluer than sky
3. the smallest ears
4. the rosiest cheeks
5. the prettiest smile

Only one starlet had all of these things. She got the part. Who was it?

Ruby Stone

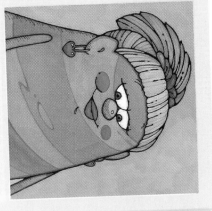

River Jade

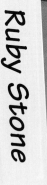

Pebble Shore

Sandy Rock

4

5

Sound Makers

8

2

Sweetly Sings the Farmer

"Amazingly fine sound effects!"
–*The Weekly Reporter*

A farmer carefully mows the hay. Here is how the sound was made.

Sound effects are cleverly made to make you think you hear what is happening in the film. Let's see how the filmmaker made some of the sound effects for *Sweetly Sings the Farmer*.

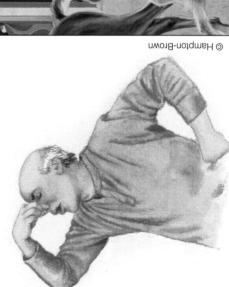

3

A pig oinks loudly for its meal. Here is how the sound was made.

6

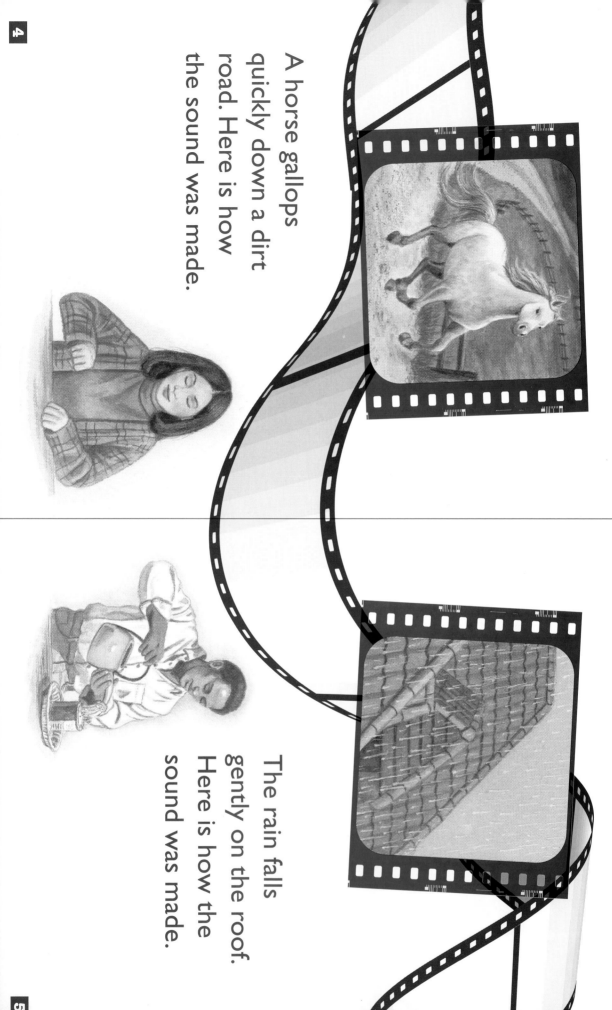

A horse gallops quickly down a dirt road. Here is how the sound was made.

The rain falls gently on the roof. Here is how the sound was made.

4

5

NEVER GIVE UP!

© Hampton-Brown

The Hopeless Hounds
ful

starring
Powerful Pup

The Hope**ful** Hounds

Starring
Powerful Pup

"A cheerful romp from beginning to end!"
–*The Noseful News*

7. Powerful Pup tries one more time.
He makes a flawless kick.

8. Powerful Pup scores! Joyful fans roar,
"Hooray for the HopeFUL Hounds!"